PAINTINGS AND SCULPTURE

from the

MELLON COLLECTION

NATIONAL GALLERY OF ART

SMITHSONIAN INSTITUTION

WASHINGTON, D. C.

First Printing, November 1949
Second Printing, August 1953

FOREWORD

M R. MELLON began, as most collectors do, by buying an occasional painting because he liked it and wished to have it in his house where he could enjoy it.

He was influenced in the beginning by his friend, Mr. Henry Clay Frick, with whom as a young man he first visited Europe. Mr. Mellon once told me that the first painting which he bought cost a thousand dollars; and I have been told by others that this was considered by his friends in Pittsburgh an unaccountable aberration in a young man of such sound judgment in all matters relating to business. But Mr. Mellon persisted; and he and his friend, Mr. Frick, continued to buy paintings, which later they exchanged for finer ones as their available funds increased.

At first Mr. Mellon bought paintings by English and Dutch masters. He liked instinctively Rembrandt, Vermeer, Hals, and Hobbema; and something in his British and Irish ancestry seemed to make him feel at home among Gainsboroughs, Reynolds, Romneys, Raeburns, and Constables. In later years his dining room at 1785 Massachusetts Avenue in Washington was filled with portraits such as those of Miss Urquhart, Miss Willoughby, John Tait and his grandson; and surrounded by such agreeable, if silent, company, Mr. Mellon felt quite happy, even when dining alone.

He had certain standards from which he never deviated. A painting must be by an outstanding artist; it must be in good condition; and it must be beautiful or pleasant to look at. He did not like dark pictures, especially those with black backgrounds; and he had an aversion to paintings depicting unpleasant or harrowing scenes. He visited art galleries and private collections whenever he could and had definite ideas as to the artists whose work he wished to include in his collection. He had an excellent eye and could recognize quality in a painting, whether by a celebrated or a minor master. His decision to buy was based solely on whether he liked the picture or not; and in coming to his decision he was neither influenced by snobbish considerations nor deterred by the price, if he thought the picture was worth it.

He bought from only two or three dealers whom he had known for many years and in whom he had confidence. When they had a painting they thought he might wish to acquire, they usually brought it to Washington and hung it in Mr. Mellon's rooms in the hope that he would become accustomed to it and like it so much that in the end he would buy it, as he often did, but not always. Once he returned to the dealer a fine portrait by Raphael, merely because the painting did not give him pleasure. At that time his collection contained no work by this master, although eventually Mr. Mellon was to acquire three paintings by Raphael, including the incomparable *Saint George and the Dragon*. Later Mr. Mellon's concept of his collection changed when he determined that it should become the nucleus of a national collection.

When he came to Washington in 1921 as Secretary of the Treasury, he found there no Government-owned museum with a comprehensive collection of paintings and sculpture by the greatest masters, such as could be found in other world capitals of comparable importance. In the opinion of Mr. Mellon, the time had come when America must have at the seat of Government in Washington a National Gallery of which all Americans could be proud. He determined to provide a building and to give the works of art which he had collected to form the nucleus of what he hoped would some day become a great national collection. These works were not to be segregated but were to be shown, with others that might come in the future, in such a way that the public could obtain the maximum benefit and pleasure in seeing them.

Mr. Mellon first came to this decision, so far as I know, about 1927. Thereafter he tried to build up his collection in such a way that it would illustrate the principal changes in direction, style, and taste in the field of Western painting, beginning with the Byzantine Madonna of c. 1200, and ending with the Constables and Turners that foreshadow the Impressionists of nineteenth-century France.

Mr. Mellon seized the opportunity when it came to him to buy twenty-one celebrated paintings which had then come on the market from the Hermitage Gallery in Leningrad; and less than twelve months before his death, he bought in one fabulous acquisition twenty-six paintings of the greatest importance, ranging from works by Cimabue and Masaccio to Gainsborough's *Landscape with a Bridge*. He also acquired in this purchase most of the sculpture now in the Mellon Collection, including famous works by Donatello, Verrocchio, Desiderio da Settignano, and others.

Mr. Mellon had not at first intended to include sculpture in the National Gallery of Art. The ideal art gallery, in his opinion, was the National Gallery in London, which he admired not only for the high standard of quality maintained throughout its collection of paintings, but also for its homogeneity and lack of confusion in the objects shown. When the opportunity arose, however, to acquire rare and famous sculptures from the Dreyfus, Morgan, Ryan, and other collections, Mr. Mellon determined to do so, realizing that in Washington there were no collections of sculpture such as could be found in the British Museum and the Victoria and Albert Museum in London. Mr. Mellon was also of the opinion that it was important for the American people to become familiar with achievements in the field of sculpture, as well as in painting.

Furthermore, he felt that it was of primary importance that America's National Gallery should contain a representative collection of the finest examples obtainable of American painting. To this end he bought the Clarke Collection of American portraits with the intention that a few of aesthetic value, such as Gilbert Stuart's famous portrait of Mrs. Yates, should go to the National Gallery. Portraits of historic American personages he intended for a National Portrait Gallery, which he hoped to organize for the purpose of promoting patriotism and a better understanding of American history. These portraits are now held by the Trustees of the National Gallery of Art until such time as they can be installed and shown in a National Portrait Gallery in Washington.

The last work of art which Mr. Mellon acquired came only a few weeks before his death. It was Duccio's *Nativity* from the Maestà of Siena, exchanged by the Kaiser Friedrich Museum in Berlin for another painting in order to placate Hitler's craving for what he considered "German" art.

Mr. Mellon did not live to see the realization of his dream of a great National Gallery which should be a joint undertaking by the Federal Government on the one hand, and by generous-minded individuals on the other, who would give works of art or funds with which to buy them, so that eventually the National Gallery at Washington could take its place with the other important galleries of the world.

The beautiful, white marble building, which was built with funds provided by Mr. Mellon, was begun shortly before his death and was subsequently completed under the direction of Paul Mellon, Donald D. Shepard, and David K. E. Bruce, Trustees of the A. W. Mellon Educational and Charitable Trust.

Since Mr. Mellon's death many great gifts have come to the National Gallery from other generous donors and have rounded out the Nation's collection to a degree and with a rapidity that could not have been anticipated when the Gallery was established. As a result the National Gallery of Art, in the quality and scope of its collections, ranks today with the six or seven greatest art museums in the world.

The National Gallery is now equipped to do the two things for which it was created: first, to set up and maintain a standard of quality by collecting, preserving and exhibiting to the best advantage the finest works of art obtainable in the fields of Western painting, sculpture, and the graphic arts; and second, to make those works of art known and enjoyed by the people of the United States of America to whom they belong.

More than a million people visit the National Gallery each year, coming from all parts of the United States and the world. Thus in the short space of eight years the National Gallery has become one of the really potent forces in this country not only to increase knowledge and improve taste, but also to give to our own people the elements of a democratic culture, based on idealism and a discriminating sense of values in the field of the arts.

DAVID E. FINLEY

Director

INTRODUCTION

IT WAS the destiny of the Mellon Collection to provide a framework on which the collections of the National Gallery of Art have grown. Leaving aside for the moment the distinguished group of sculpture, Mr. Mellon's contribution to the Gallery recapitulates the development of Western painting. His gift begins with a Byzantine Madonna of the thirteenth century and ends with a Turner landscape of the nineteenth century. Between these terminal paintings there is an example by almost every artist who strongly affected the development of style. Though Mr. Mellon's collection contains only one hundred and fifteen pictures, exclusive of American portraits, these were chosen with such discrimination that they provide a nearly complete outline of eight centuries of European painting.

The Byzantine Madonna, already mentioned, illustrates the source of Italian art and, to a large extent, of all European art. The fulfillment of this Byzantine mode of representation was reached in Siena. The Mellon Collection shows an example of its climactic achievement, a panel by Duccio di Buoninsegna from the Maestà of that city. This fragment of the predella was, until sold by Hitler, one of the greatest treasures of the Kaiser Friedrich Museum. The final embellishments and transformations of the Byzantine tradition also appear in the work of other Sienese artists, many of whom are represented in the Mellon Collection: Lippo Memmi, Giovanni di Paolo, Neroccio de' Landi, Matteo and Benvenuto di Giovanni.

The revolt against the Byzantine style, which characterized the more progressive movement of the fourteenth century, is also illustrated. Though this newer style is barely suggested in the earliest Florentine painting, the triptych by Cimabue, which is still Byzantine in its austere formalism, the first break with the past is evident in a slightly later panel, a majestic figure of St. Paul, so close to Giotto as to have been often ascribed to him. Here one sees that passionate quest for solidity and massiveness which was to be the major goal of so much Florentine painting—an aesthetic end concisely described more than a century later in

Leonardo da Vinci's axiom: "The first object of the painter is to make a flat plane appear as a body in relief and projecting from that plane."

After the death of Giotto Florentine artists for a time lost sight of this objective. They were seduced by a love of accessories, by a desire to represent rich stuffs for their own richness, graceful gestures for their own grace, to forget form for pattern. This attractive heresy is charmingly illustrated in the Mellon Collection by triptychs by Agnolo Gaddi and the Umbro-Florentines, Allegretto Nuzi and the Fabriano Master.

At the beginning of the fifteenth century, however, Florentine artists were recalled to the true faith by a fanatic of form, Tommaso di Ser Giovanni Guidi, called Masaccio. Dying at twenty-seven, he left as one of his earliest works the *Madonna and Child* of the Mellon Collection. It shows Our Blessed Lady seated like some hieratic image from Egypt or Yucatan, serene and immobile, as though carved from a monolith. The contrast between two other Florentine paintings of almost as early a date, one also by Masaccio, the other by a slightly later contemporary, Domenico Veneziano, indicates how easily plastic form, like quicksilver, can slip through the fingers of artists. In the *Profile Portrait of a Young Man,* a second panel in the Mellon Collection by Masaccio, the convex forms of the face are suggested with the most delicate gradations of modelling, whereas in the profile by Domenico Veneziano painted a few years later these forms have lost their density and instead of seeming carved in relief look as though they had been beaten out in *repoussé* work.

These two portraits also point to the growing interest of the Renaissance in the individual, in the outward semblance of personality. In the Mellon Collection are a number of unforgettable faces, studies in physiognomy which are among the greatest achievements of portraiture. The epitome of the Renaissance intellectual, for example, is to be found in Antonio Pollaiuolo's portrait of an unknown man, a face of cruel sensuousness but of immense intellectual vitality; or, at the other extreme, the ideal of adolescent loveliness is caught in two portraits of young boys, one with a tired, wistful beauty, by Botticelli, the other calmly self-assured, by Filippino Lippi. Characterizations just as penetrating come from further north in the portraits of women by Pisanello and Luini, and of men by Antonello da Messina, Giovanni Bellini, and Titian.

Portraiture was one aspect of the preoccupying interest of the Renaissance in reality, using this term in its broadest sense. A similar interest resulted in a long struggle to make three-dimensional objects seem to move. The Mellon Collection does not illustrate all the steps by which figures ceased to be static and gradually achieved mobility, but the *Adoration of the Magi* by Botticelli shows one of the peaks of this development. From the calmness of the center, from the mystical yet human serenity of the Madonna and Child, movement radiates through the gestures of wonder and of prayer of the onlookers and reaches a climax in the youthful grooms who with difficulty restrain their impatient horses.

The landscape background in Botticelli's panel introduces another problem brilliantly solved by Renaissance painters—the relation between man and his environment and its corollary, the composition of objects in space. Perugino's altarpiece, *The Crucifixion with Saints,* is a perfect though simple solution of the interrelation of figures and background, with the saints symmetrically placed in the first plane, an enframement of high cliffs at either side, and a deep space in the center into which the eye glides to the remote horizon. Two of the three paintings by Raphael in the Mellon Collection offer more complex solutions and also show the extraordinary increase in naturalism that comes in one generation. Especially noteworthy is the *Saint George and the Dragon,* perhaps the most perfectly preserved panel by Raphael in existence. The reality of the roadway passing under tall trees and the clarity of light falling on hills, meadows and a distant city show to what extent observation had increased. But Raphael was to go still further, and with the famous *Alba Madonna* he seems to portray a particular place, here the upper reaches of the Tiber near Orvieto.

Though the Mellon Collection illustrates particularly well the painting of Florence and her artistic dependency, Umbria, it also includes superb examples of the North Italian Schools—portraits and religious subjects by Mantegna, Luini, Cima, Giovanni Bellini, Antonello da Messina, Titian, and Paolo Veronese. The connection between these painters who worked in North Italy and artists in Burgundy, Flanders, and Germany was close. For example, the *Portrait of a Lady* ascribed to Pisanello has been considered by a number of critics a product of the Burgundian School; we know that Albrecht Dürer worked in Venice, and whether or not he painted the *Portrait of a Man* tentatively ascribed to him in the Mellon Collection, this panel is the work of an artist familiar with Venetian painting; and Antonello da Messina, according to Vasari, went to Bruges and became intimate with Jan van Eyck, who, "moved by the respect shown by Antonello, and being now old, was content that he should see his (van Eyck's) method of painting in oil." The luminosity of the two panels by Antonello in the Mellon Collection is doubtless due to this new technical knowledge which was brought from Flanders to Venice.

For in the technique of panel painting the Flemish artists of the fifteenth century were in advance of their Italian colleagues. In a few supremely beautiful examples the Mellon Collection illustrates the style of this northern school, which was established almost single handed by the work of Jan van Eyck. Of paramount importance is the *Annunciation* by van Eyck himself. It shows his salient characteristics: his masterful suggestion of atmosphere through subtle gradations of light and his immense skill in rendering detail. From the half-visible frescoes in the dimly lit clerestory of the church to the hard, microscopic clarity of the jewels in the angel's robe, there is a range of representation unequalled in the work of any other artist.

Nor has any other painter established, by the example of his own work alone, so creative a school as that of Jan van Eyck. Every fifteenth-century Flemish artist is in a sense his pupil. The brilliance of this school can be judged by the work of four of the greatest of the van Eyck disciples, Rogier van der Weyden, Petrus Christus, Hans Memling, and Gerard David, who are all represented by splendid panels in the Mellon Collection.

The sixteenth century in the north, which was a less creative period than the preceding century, is represented in the Mellon Collection by Miguel Sithium's *Knight of the Order of Calatrava,* Antonis Mor's *Portrait of a Gentleman* and Holbein's *Edward VI as a Child* and his *Sir Brian Tuke,* all works of the greatest distinction. Two paintings by another non-Italian artist of the sixteenth century in the Mellon Collection should also be mentioned—El Greco's *Saint Martin and the Beggar* and his *Saint Ildefonso,* which once belonged to Degas, are brilliant links with modern painting.

Apart from the work of Italian artists, the greatest masterpieces in Mr. Mellon's gift are by seventeenth-century painters. The three leading schools of this period, which were located in Flanders, Holland, and Spain, have all a remarkable representation. Of the Grand Manner in portraiture there are a series of paintings by Van Dyck from his Flemish,

Italian, and English periods. They illustrate the change which took place in the artist's social position between the time when he painted in Genoa such portraits as the *Marchesa Balbi* and the much later period in England, when he painted *Philip, Lord Wharton*. In the first of these portraits there is a formality which indicates a certain awe on the part of the painter toward his sitter, with the Marchesa seeming to tower above him, aloof and remote; in the second, the portraitist and his sitter are on familiar terms, and Lord Wharton is shown at eye level, with as much informality as seventeenth-century taste permitted. Yet in both portraits how brilliantly Van Dyck embodies our conception of the great lady and the great gentleman!

Though hung in adjacent galleries, the aristocratic art of Flanders and the bourgeois art of Holland are separated by an immense distance. In Dutch painting the Mellon Collection reaches its climax. The nine Rembrandts, mostly from the Hermitage Gallery in Leningrad, show the full development of the greatest of all Dutch artists, from *A Turk*, painted in the early 1630's, to the *Lucretia*, of 1664. Among these masterful canvases perhaps the most moving is the portrait of Rembrandt himself, as he looked toward the end of his life, when time and misfortune had left their marks in the deep lines of his face. His tired and saddened eyes seem weary not only of his insight into others but also of his knowledge of himself. For he has not spared his own faults: his weak chin and sensuous mouth indicate those flaws of character which contributed to the tragedy of his life.

All the other Dutch painters belong to a different world—a world in which the tragic destiny of human beings is ignored, either in a constant carnival of drinking and love-making or in the calm felicity of domestic happiness. These minor masters of Dutch painting—Ter Borch, Metsu, and de Hooch—are represented in the Mellon Collection each by a single well-chosen work. The landscapists, too, Hobbema and Cuyp appear, Cuyp with two canvases and Hobbema with four.

But after Rembrandt the greatest masters of the Dutch School were not these artists, but Frans Hals and Jan Vermeer of Delft. Compared to Rembrandt's portraits the Hals sitters are easily pigeonholed in broad and obvious categories. However, his five canvases in the Mellon Collection will always appeal to those who love painting for its own sake, who enjoy the sword play of the brush, the rapid staccato touch which renders form with a few brilliant strokes.

In place of the dashing, impressionistic brushwork of Frans Hals, the three paintings by Jan Vermeer of Delft show a meticulous and careful touch. Whereas with Hals the sitter is seen at a quick glance, with Vermeer he is seen with a steady gaze. One suggests nervous fire, the other calm stillness. These two artists represent the extremes of the Dutch rendering of form.

Perfect balance between the two methods was achieved not by a Dutch artist but by a Spaniard. In the Velázquez portraits in the Mellon Collection there is a beauty of pigmentation unsurpassed by Hals and a delicacy of handling equal to Vermeer's; but, above all, there is also an insight into character far beyond the reach of any Dutch artist except Rembrandt. And even Rembrandt distorts personality more than Velázquez, for he imposes on his sitters his own mood, his profoundly tragic attitude toward life; Velázquez shows them as they are, with an absolute detachment, leaving them with all the rich, complex variety which human nature affords. Perhaps that is why one returns again and again to the great Velázquez portraits, such as the *Innocent X,* without ever absorbing their complete meaning.

After these Titans the artists of the eighteenth century belong to a humbler, though gayer race. At the end of the eighteenth century Spain produced one last painter of genius, Goya. Two of the portraits in the Mellon Collection, the King and Queen of Spain, are replicas by the artist of larger portraits. But the others, the *Marquesa de Pontejos* and *Señora Sabasa Garcia,* are among his greatest creations. The *Marquesa de Pontejos* still belongs to the rococo period. Goya maliciously transforms his sitter into a fashion plate. Her *raison d'être* is merely to show off the artist's brilliance of handling, the virtuosity of painting in the chiffon skirt, the flowered bodice, the beribboned hat. Is there also a sly mockery of the fashionable English portrait school, whose vogue disseminated by myriads of mezzotints may have irritated Goya? In any case, *Señora Sabasa Garcia,* the other portrait, represents a radical departure from eighteenth-century formality. Here Goya has given expression to that romantic loveliness, a little mysterious and very self-assured, which appealed so strongly to nineteenth-century taste. Sabasa Garcia is a Byronic heroine who glides across the canvas so naturally and with such unaffected style that she makes the elegance of the Marchesa de Pontejos seem as posed and self-conscious as the photograph today of an Edwardian beauty.

Of the other two great eighteenth-century schools, English painting had for Mr. Mellon, as for most American collectors, a greater attraction than French painting. Thus the French section of his gift consists of only three pictures: two distinguished examples by Chardin, both of children, and a canvas by Lancret, of La Camargo dancing with her partner, once in the collection of that astute connoisseur, Frederick the Great.

The English eighteenth-century representation is as plentiful as the French is sparse. Among American collections only the Huntington Gallery in California has so many fine examples. Reynolds is represented by three full lengths, *Lady Elizabeth Compton, Lady Elizabeth Delmé and Her Children,* and *Lady Caroline Howard,* the last almost unique in its excellent preservation, for Reynolds was not a good technician and few of his portraits have retained the dewy freshness of this canvas.

Gainsborough is represented by six paintings: five portraits and one of the greatest of his landscapes. We know that Gainsborough was fond of playing the viola da gamba, and when his painting is at its best, as in all these canvases, there is a gossamer delicacy about his work, a quality as melodious as the music of that instrument.

Romney, with his fine sense of *décor,* his delicate feeling for color, is to be seen in a full length and two smaller pictures, one, *Mrs. Davenport,* his consummate masterpiece. Hoppner and Lawrence are represented by one canvas each, but the *Frankland Sisters* is among the most engaging double portraits of the time and *Lady Templeton and Her Son* among the most appealing.

There are also three portraits by Raeburn, the most beautiful of which is *Miss Eleanor Urquhart*—a miracle of direct painting, so delicately rendered that it seems breathed on the canvas.

Finally, the nineteenth century is ushered in by Constable's *View of Salisbury Cathedral* and Turner's *Mortlake Terrace* and *Approach to Venice.* These three pictures in their rendering of sunlight bring us to the threshold of the modern landscape style.

Mr. Mellon did not continue his collecting into the second half of the nineteenth century. He considered American collections to be very rich in the work of the French Impressionists and Post-Impressionists, the most significant schools of the last hundred years, and he believed that the Gallery, through gifts, would receive an ample representation of these movements—a judgment which is proving to be correct.

But American painting Mr. Mellon did wish to provide, and to that end he bought *en bloc* the Thomas B. Clarke Collection of American portraits. As Mr. Mellon realized, the quality of these portraits, almost two hundred in number and ranging from our pioneer painters to Frank Duveneck, was uneven; but he wished the National Gallery of Art and a future National Portrait Gallery to be enriched by a judicious selection from among them. Moreover, the Clarke Collection included such famous canvases as the Vaughan *Washington* and *Mrs. Richard Yates* by Gilbert Stuart, and *The Washington Family* by Savage. Mr. Mellon also made a few separate purchases to round out the American section, and with funds he provided, the Trustees of the Gallery have acquired an important work by Ryder, the only painting so far purchased from the Mellon Fund. These paintings in addition to the finest of the Clarke Collection portraits, have provided a nucleus of an American section, which has grown steadily until it has become one of the most important in the country.

Originally it was Mr. Mellon's intention to restrict his gift to painting, but he realized that to understand the development of Italian art it is necessary to know the work of the great sculptors of the Renaissance. With this in mind he concentrated on acquiring pieces of the fifteenth and sixteenth centuries, when sculpture, especially at Florence, reached one of the peaks of its development. For it was the Florentine artists under the leadership of Donatello who fused the new enthusiasm for classical art with a realism based on the observation of form and movement.

The *Madonna and Child* in the Mellon Collection by Donatello has this progressive character, as has that superb terra-cotta study, possibly for a fountain, the running putto by Verrocchio. This tradition reaches its final expression in the sixteenth century in the Mercury by Giovanni da Bologna and the bronze statues by Sansovino.

Like the painters of the Quattrocento, the sculptors were also preoccupied with problems of human personality. Some of the greatest pieces in the Mellon Collection are the superlatively realized portraits, beginning with the Florentine youth in the guise of Saint John by Donatello and continuing with the enchanting study of childhood by Desiderio da Settignano, the Sforza reliefs by Amadeo, the bust of an Aragonese princess by that precursor of Brancusi, Francesco Laurana, and ending with an incisive characterization by Verrocchio of Giuliano de' Medici, brother of Lorenzo the Magnificent.

Among other examples of carving, religious in subject matter, there are in the Mellon Collection two allegorical figures by Mino da Fiesole, which rise far above his usual level, and two exquisite pieces by that master of low relief, Desiderio da Settignano. But perhaps the most fascinating example of religious sculpture given by Mr. Mellon is the *Madonna and Child* by a recherché master of sculptural line, Agostino di Duccio, who worked principally for Sigismondo Malatesta at Rimini. It would be hard to find elsewhere an interpretation of Our Lady so surprisingly malevolent, so subtly wicked as she appears in this relief. One explanation might be that Agostino was inspired by the features of his principal patroness, one of the most enthralling but also one of the most baneful women of the Renaissance, the mistress of Sigismondo Malatesta, Isotta degli Atti, for whose sake her lover was excommunicated and his city state laid under interdict.

Like the collection of paintings, the number of pieces of sculpture bought by Mr. Mellon is small, just over a score, to which the Trustees of the A. W. Mellon Educational and Charitable Trust have added two marble urns by Clodion and two fountains, one by Tubi and the other by Legros. But in both painting and sculpture the quality of the works of art shows the most exacting connoisseurship. Mr. Mellon wished his collection to establish a measuring rod, which would guide future trustees in their acceptance of gifts for the Gallery. Thus he set himself the difficult task of acquiring nothing but masterpieces, an undertaking which can fail with even the greatest financial resources. Mr. Mellon, however, succeeded, as the reader will be able to judge from the reproductions on the following pages. Unfortunately, he did not live to see his collection installed in the National Gallery. Thus he did not witness and enjoy that moment, which would have meant so much to him, when, with all his pictures and sculpture in place, he might have said to himself in Louis MacNeill's words,

"Hundreds of windows are open again on a vital but changeless world — a daydream free from doubt."

JOHN WALKER

Chief Curator

April 18, 1949

xvii

ITALIAN PAINTINGS

Wood   32⅛ x 19⅜ in.

1   Enthroned Madonna and Child
BYZANTINE SCHOOL. XIII CENTURY

— 3 —

Center: 17¼ x 17½ in.

8   *Nativity with Isaiah and Ezekiel*
   DUCCIO DI BUONINSEGNA
   Sienese. Active 1278-1319

Wood

2 *Christ Between Saint Peter and Saint James Major*

CIMABUE

Florentine. Mentioned 1272-1302

Wood

Center: 31 x 21¾ in.

Wood   22¼ x 9½ in.

11   Madonna and Child with Donor
LIPPO MEMMI
Sienese. Active 1317-1347

Wood   92 x 35⅛ in.

3   *Saint Paul*
FOLLOWER OF GIOTTO
Italian. First Half XIV Century

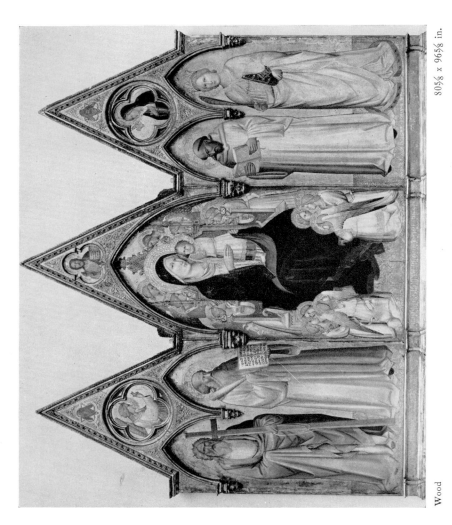

Wood

80⅝ x 96⅝ in.

4 *Madonna and Child with Saints and Angels*

AGNOLO GADDI

Florentine. Active 1366-1396

6 *Madonna Enthroned with Saints*

ALLEGRETTO NUZI AND MASTER OF THE FABRIANO ALTARPIECE

School of Fabriano. Active 1346-1373/74 and c. 1350 respectively

Wood — Center: 42¾ x 23⅜ in.

MATHEVS OLIVIERI DÑI IOANNI FILI

Transferred from wood to canvas   18⅞ x 13 5⁄16 in.

15   *Matteo Olivieri*
Domenico Veneziano
Florentine. c. 1400-1461

Wood   165⁄8 x 123⁄4 in.

14   *Profile Portrait of a Young Man*
MASACCIO
Florentine. 1401-1427/28

Wood   41⅜ x 21⅛ in.

7   *The Madonna of Humility*
MASACCIO
Florentine. 1401-1427/28

Wood   20⅜ x 14⅜ in.

23   Profile Portrait of a Lady
P<small>ISANELLO</small>
School of Verona. c. 1395-1455

Wood   58¼ x 45¼ in.

16   The Annunciation
MASOLINO DA PANICALE
Florentine. 1384-c. 1435

Wood

24 x 17⅞ in.

5   *The Madonna of Humility*
FRA ANGELICO
Florentine. 1387-1455

10¼ x 17¾ in.

Wood

13   *The Adoration of the Magi*
GIOVANNI DI PAOLO
Sienese. 1403-1482

Wood

713/4 x 541/8 in.

10   *The Adoration of the Magi*
Benvenuto di Giovanni
Sienese. 1436-c. 1518

Wood   41¼ x 18 3/16 in.

12   *Claudia Quinta*
NEROCCIO DE' LANDI AND MASTER OF THE GRISELDA LEGEND
Sienese. 1447-1500 and Active End of XV Century respectively

— 18 —

Wood

31 x 23 in.

9   *Madonna and Child with Angels and Cherubim*
MATTEO DI GIOVANNI
Sienese. c. 1430-1495

Wood   16 x 12 in.

19   Portrait of a Youth
BOTTICELLI
Florentine. 1444-1510

Wood

21 $\frac{5}{16}$ x 15⅞ in.

17   *Portrait of a Man*
ANTONIO POLLAIUOLO
Florentine. 1432-1498

Wood   32 x 22⅛ in.

18   The Adoration of the Child
FILIPPINO LIPPI
Florentine. 1457-1504

Wood   20 x 13⅞ in.

20   Portrait of a Youth
FILIPPINO LIPPI
Florentine. 1457-1504

— 23 —

Wood

27⅝ x 41 in.

22   *The Adoration of the Magi*
BOTTICELLI
Florentine. 1444-1510

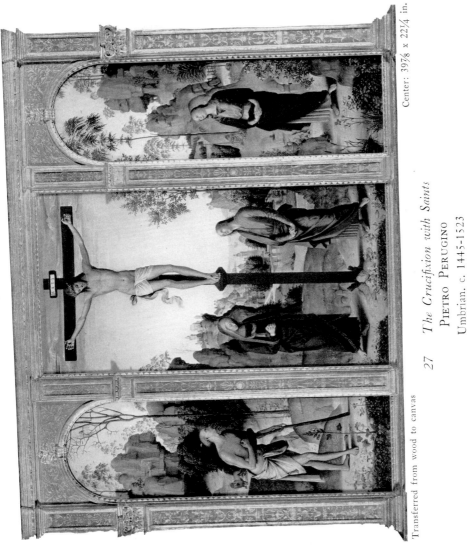

Transferred from wood to canvas

27 *The Crucifixion with Saints*
PIETRO PERUGINO
Umbrian. c. 1445-1523

Center: 39⅞ x 22¼ in.

Wood   29⅞ x 21⅞ in.

21   Madonna and Child
BOTTICELLI
Florentine. 1444-1510

Wood

$11\frac{1}{8}$ x $8\frac{7}{16}$ in.

26   Saint George and the Dragon
RAPHAEL
Umbrian. 1483-1520

Wood   31¾ x 22⅝ in.

25   The Niccolini-Cowper Madonna
RAPHAEL
Umbrian. 1483-1520

Transferred from wood to canvas

Diam. 37¼ in.

24 *The Alba Madonna*
RAPHAEL
Umbrian. 1483-1520

Wood   31¾ x 21⅝ in.

32   Saint Jerome in the Wilderness
ANDREA MANTEGNA
Paduan. 1431-1506

Wood   23¼ x 17¼ in.

30   *Madonna and Child*
ANTONELLO DA MESSINA
Sicilian. 1430-1479

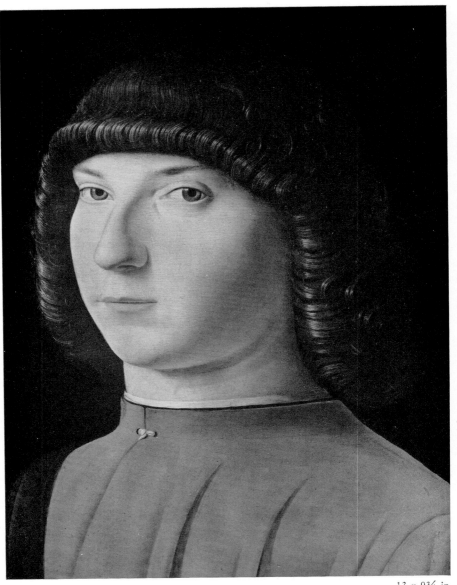

Wood

13 x 9¾ in.

31   Portrait of a Young Man
ANTONELLO DA MESSINA
Sicilian. 1430-1479

Wood   12½ x 10⅜ in.

29   *Portrait of a Young Man in Red*
GIOVANNI BELLINI
Venetian. c. 1430-1516

28   *The Flight into Egypt*
GIOVANNI BELLINI
Venetian. c. 1430-1516

28¼ x 43⅞ in.

Wood

Wood

41⅛ x 57⅝ in.

33   Madonna and Child with Saints

CIMA DA CONEGLIANO

Venetian. c. 1459-1517/18

Wood   30⅜ x 22⁹⁄₁₆ in.

37   Portrait of a Lady
BERNARDINO LUINI
Milanese. c. 1480-1532

Canvas

25½ x 20 in.

35   *Andrea dei Franceschi*
TITIAN
Venetian. c. 1477-1576

Canvas   49 x 41½ in.

34   Venus with a Mirror
TITIAN
Venetian. c. 1477-1576

Canvas   22¾ x 17½ in.

38   *The Finding of Moses*
PAOLO VERONESE
Venetian. 1528-1588

Canvas

11 x 22¾ in.

36   *Madonna and Child and the Infant Saint John*

TITIAN

Venetian. c. 1477-1576

SPANISH PAINTINGS

Canvas   44¼ x 25¾ in.

83   *Saint Ildefonso*

EL GRECO

Spanish. 1541-1614

Canvas   41 x 23⅝ in.

84   *Saint Martin and the Beggar*
EL GRECO
Spanish. 1541-1614

Canvas   19½ x 16¼ in.

80   *Pope Innocent X*
DIEGO VELÁZQUEZ DE SILVA
Spanish. 1599-1660

Canvas   23¼ x 18⅞ in.

82   Portrait of a Young Man
DIEGO VELÁZQUEZ DE SILVA
Spanish. 1599-1660

Canvas   29⅛ x 23⅝ in.

81   The Needlewoman
DIEGO VELÁZQUEZ DE SILVA
Spanish. 1599-1660

Canvas   28 x 23 in.

88   Señora Sabasa Garcia
FRANCISCO JOSÉ DE GOYA Y LUCIENTES
Spanish. 1746-1828

Canvas   18¼ x 11¾ in.

86   Carlos IV of Spain as Huntsman
FRANCISCO JOSÉ DE GOYA Y LUCIENTES
Spanish. 1746-1828

Canvas

18¼ x 11¾ in.

87 *Maria Luisa, Queen of Spain*
FRANCISCO JOSÉ DE GOYA Y LUCIENTES
Spanish. 1746-1828

Canvas   83 x 49¾ in.

85   Marquesa de Pontejos
Francisco José de Goya y Lucientes
Spanish. 1746-1828

EARLY FLEMISH PAINTINGS

Transferred from wood to canvas   36½ x 14⅜ in.

39 The Annunciation

JAN VAN EYCK

Flemish. 1380/1400-1441

Wood   51¼ x 38¼ in.

40   The Nativity
PETRUS CHRISTUS
Flemish. c. 1410-1472/73

Wood   64 x 36⅝ in.

45   *Christ Appearing to the Virgin*
ROGIER VAN DER WEYDEN
Flemish. 1399/1400-1464

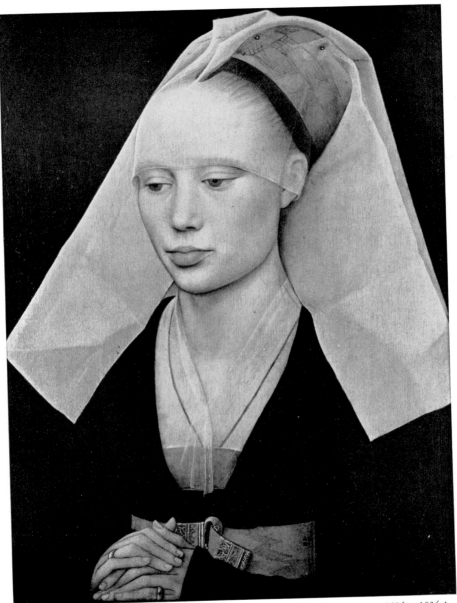

Wood

14½ x 10¾ in.

44   Portrait of a Lady
ROGIER VAN DER WEYDEN
Flemish. 1399/1400-1464

Wood   17¾ x 17½ in.

43   The Rest on the Flight into Egypt
GERARD DAVID
Flemish. c. 1460-1523

Wood

23⅛ x 18⅞ in.

41   Madonna and Child with Angels
HANS MEMLING
Flemish. 1430/35-1494

Wood   12⅝ x 10¼ in.

42   *A Man with an Arrow*
HANS MEMLING
Flemish. 1430/35-1494

Wood

$13\frac{3}{16}$ x $9\frac{5}{16}$ in.

46   A Knight of the Order of Calatrava
MIGUEL SITHIUM
Flemish. c. 1465/70-1525

GERMAN PAINTINGS

Wood   15⅝ x 12⅝ in.

66   Portrait of a Man
ALBRECHT DÜRER (?)
German. 1471-1528

Wood   19⅜ x 15¼ in.

65   *Sir Brian Tuke*
HANS HOLBEIN, THE YOUNGER
German. 1497-1543

PARVVLE PATRISSA, PATRIÆ VIRTVTIS ET HÆRES
ESTO, NIHIL MAIVS MAXIMVS ORBIS HABET.
GNATVM VIX POSSVNT COELVM ET NATVRA DEDISSE,
HVIVS QVEM PATRIS, VICTVS HONORET HONOS.
ÆQVATO TANTVM, TANTI TV FACTA PARENTIS,
VOTA HOMINVM, VIX QVO PROGREDIANTVR, HABENT
VINCITO, VICISTI, QVOT REGES PRISCVS ADORAT
ORBIS, NEC TE QVI VINCERE POSSIT, ERIT.

Wood   22⅜ x 17⅜ in.

64   Edward VI as a Child
HANS HOLBEIN, THE YOUNGER
German. 1497-1543

LATER FLEMISH PAINTINGS

Transferred from wood to canvas   47⅛ x 34¾ in.

52   Portrait of a Gentleman
ANTONIS MOR
Flemish-Dutch. 1519-1575

Canvas

48⅜ x 35½ in.

500 Portrait of a Flemish Lady
Sir Anthony Van Dyck
Flemish. 1599-1641

Canvas   60¼ x 47¼ in.

47   *Isabella Brant*
PETER PAUL RUBENS
Flemish. 1577-1640

Canvas   68 x 46¼ in.

48   Susanna Fourment and her Daughter
SIR ANTHONY VAN DYCK
Flemish. 1599-1641

Canvas   72 x 48 in.

49   Marchesa Balbi
SIR ANTHONY VAN DYCK
Flemish. 1599-1641

Canvas

52½ x 41⅞ in.

50   *Philip, Lord Wharton*
SIR ANTHONY VAN DYCK
Flemish. 1599-1641

Canvas   41¼ x 34¼ in.

51   William II of Nassau and Orange
SIR ANTHONY VAN DYCK
Flemish. 1599-1641

DUTCH PAINTINGS

Canvas   40¼ x 34 in.

67   Portrait of an Elderly Lady
FRANS HALS
Dutch. c. 1580-1666

Wood

11½ x 9⅛ in.

498   A Young Man in a Large Hat
FRANS HALS
Dutch. c. 1580-1666

Canvas   33¾ x 27 in.

68   Portrait of an Officer
FRANS HALS
Dutch. c. 1580-1666

Canvas

30¼ x 25 in.

69   *Balthasar Coymans*
FRANS HALS
Dutch. c. 1580-1666

Canvas   26⅞ x 21⅞ in.

71   *Portrait of a Young Man*
FRANS HALS
Dutch. c. 1580-1666

Canvas

37 x 29½ in.

70   *Portrait of a Man*
FRANS HALS
Dutch. c. 1580-1666

Wood

38⅛ x 26 in.

78   *A Polish Nobleman*
Rembrandt van Ryn
Dutch. 1606-1669

Canvas   38¾ x 29⅛ in.

499   A Turk
REMBRANDT VAN RYN
Dutch. 1606-1669

Canvas   42¼ x 36 in.

74   A Girl with a Broom
REMBRANDT VAN RYN
Dutch. 1606-1669

Canvas 43 x 36 in.

73 *An Old Lady with a Book*
REMBRANDT VAN RYN
Dutch. 1606-1669

Canvas   47¼ x 39¾ in.

76   Lucretia

REMBRANDT VAN RYN

Dutch. 1606-1669

Canvas

415⁄8 x 38½ in.

79   *Joseph Accused by Potiphar's Wife*
REMBRANDT VAN RYN
Dutch. 1606-1669

Canvas   40⅜ x 33¾ in.

75   *A Woman Holding a Pink*
REMBRANDT VAN RYN
Dutch. 1606-1669

Canvas

33¼ x 26 in.

72   *Self-Portrait*
REMBRANDT VAN RYN
Dutch. 1606-1669

Canvas   43¼ x 35¼ in.

77   *A Young Man Seated at a Table*
REMBRANDT VAN RYN
Dutch. 1606-1669

Canvas   32⅜ x 26⅜ in.

63   An Old Woman Dozing Over a Book
Nicolas Maes
Dutch. 1632-1693

Wood   26¼ x 23½ in.

57   The Intruder
GABRIEL METSU
Dutch. c. 1629-1667

Canvas

31½ x 29⅝ in.

58   *The Suitor's Visit*
GERARD TER BORCH
Dutch. 1617-1681

Canvas

$26\frac{3}{4}$ x $23\frac{1}{16}$ in.

56   A Dutch Courtyard
PIETER DE HOOCH
Dutch. 1629-c. 1683

Canvas   17½ x 15¾ in.

54   *The Lacemaker*
JAN VERMEER
Dutch. 1632-1675

Wood   9⅛ x 7⅛ in.

Canvas   16⅛ x 12½ in.

55   *The Smiling Girl*
JAN VERMEER
Dutch. 1632-1675

Canvas   26 x 34½ in.

59   *Herdsmen Tending Cattle*
AELBERT CUYP
Dutch. 1620-1691

Canvas

$45\frac{1}{4}$ x 67 in.

501   *The Maas at Dordrecht*

AELBERT CUYP

Dutch. 1620-1691

Canvas

37½ x 51⅜ in.

61   *A Wooded Landscape*
MEINDERT HOBBEMA
Dutch. 1638-1709

Canvas

36¾ x 50½ in

62   *A View on a High Road*
Meindert Hobbema
Dutch. 1638-1709

Canvas   32 x 25⅞ in.

60   A Farm in the Sunlight
MEINDERT HOBBEMA
Dutch. 1638-1709

FRENCH PAINTINGS

Canvas

30 x 42 in.

89   *La Camargo Dancing*

NICOLAS LANCRET

French. 1690-1743

91   The Young Governess
JEAN-BAPTISTE-SIMÉON CHARDIN
French. 1699-1779

Canvas

23 x 29¼ in.

Canvas   32⅜ x 26 in.

90   The House of Cards
JEAN-BAPTISTE-SIMÉON CHARDIN
French. 1699-1779

ENGLISH PAINTINGS

Canvas   94 x 58⅛ in.

95   *Lady Elizabeth Delmé and Her Children*
SIR JOSHUA REYNOLDS
British. 1723-1792

Canvas   56¼ x 44½ in.

106   Lady Caroline Howard
SIR JOSHUA REYNOLDS
British. 1723-1792

Canvas   94½ x 58½ in.

97   Lady Elizabeth Compton
S<small>IR</small> J<small>OSHUA</small> R<small>EYNOLDS</small>
British. 1723-1792

Canvas   92¾ x 57½ in.

93   Georgiana, Duchess of Devonshire
THOMAS GAINSBOROUGH
British. 1727-1788

Canvas   30⅛ x 24⅞ in.

98   *George IV as Prince of Wales*
THOMAS GAINSBOROUGH
British. 1727-1788

Canvas

30 x 25 in.

100   Mrs. John Taylor
THOMAS GAINSBOROUGH
British. 1727-1788

Canvas   30 x 25 in.

99   Miss Catherine Tatton
THOMAS GAINSBOROUGH
British. 1727-1788

Canvas   86½ x 60½ in.

92   *Mrs. Richard Brinsley Sheridan*
Thomas Gainsborough
British. 1727-1788

Canvas   94 x 58 in.

94   Lady Broughton
GEORGE ROMNEY
British. 1734-1802

— 114 —

Canvas

36⅛ x 28 in.

104   *Miss Willoughby*
GEORGE ROMNEY
British. 1734-1802

Canvas

30⅛ x 25⅛ in.

105   *Mrs. Davenport*
GEORGE ROMNEY
British. 1734-1802

Canvas

29⅜ x 24¼ in.

101   Miss Eleanor Urquhart
SIR HENRY RAEBURN
British. 1756-1823

Canvas   49½ x 39¾ in.

103   *John Tait and His Grandson*
SIR HENRY RAEBURN
British. 1756-1823

Canvas

50¼ x 40 in.

102   Colonel Francis James Scott
SIR HENRY RAEBURN
British. 1756-1823

Canvas

84¾ x 58⅝ in.

96   *Lady Templeton and Her Son*
Sir Thomas Lawrence
British. 1769-1830

Canvas   61 x 49¼ in.

111   The Frankland Sisters
JOHN HOPPNER
British. 1758-1810

Canvas   44½ x 52½ in.

107   Landscape with a Bridge
THOMAS GAINSBOROUGH
British. 1727-1788

Canvas   28¾ x 36 in.

108   *A View of Salisbury Cathedral*
JOHN CONSTABLE
British. 1776-1837

Canvas

35¾ x 47½ in.

109   Mortlake Terrace
JOSEPH MALLORD WILLIAM TURNER
British. 1775-1851

Canvas

24½ x 37 in.

110   Approach to Venice
JOSEPH MALLORD WILLIAM TURNER
British. 1775–1851

AMERICAN PAINTINGS

Canvas

488   *The Washington Family*
EDWARD SAVAGE
American. 1761-1817

84 x 111¼ in.

Canvas   50¼ x 40 in.

497   Richard, Earl Howe
JOHN SINGLETON COPLEY
American. 1738-1815

793/4 x 541/2 in.

496   Colonel Guy Johnson
BENJAMIN WEST
American. 1738-1820

Canvas   50 x 40 in.

562   *John Philip de Haas*
CHARLES WILLSON PEALE
American. 1741-1827

Canvas   36 x 30 in.

574   *Sir Joshua Reynolds*

GILBERT STUART

American. 1755-1828

Canvas

30⅛ x 25 in.

487   William Vans Murray
MATHER BROWN
American. 176!-1831

Canvas

30¼ x 25⅛ in.

491   Lawrence Yates
GILBERT STUART
American. 1755–1828

Canvas

32¼ x 27⅜ in.

582   Richard Yates
GILBERT STUART
American. 1755-1828

Canvas

30¼ x 25 in.

490   *Mrs. Richard Yates*
GILBERT STUART
American. 1755-1828

Canvas

29 x 23¾ in.

580   George Washington, Vaughan Portrait
GILBERT STUART
American. 1755-1828

Canvas   29¼ x 24 in.

492   George Washington, Vaughan-Sinclair Portrait
GILBERT STUART
American. 1755-1828

Wood   35¾ x 27½ in.

570   *Commodore Thomas Macdonough*
GILBERT STUART
American. 1755-1828

Canvas

29⅛ x 24⅛ in.

495   *John Randolph*
GILBERT STUART
American. 1755-1828

Canvas

28⅛ x 22¾ in.

489   Joseph Coolidge
GILBERT STUART
American. 1755-1828

Canvas

30¼ x 24¼ in.

494   Alexander Hamilton
JOHN TRUMBULL
American. 1756-1843

Canvas   35⅝ x 27⅜ in.

584   Major Thomas Biddle
THOMAS WILCOCKS SULLY AND THOMAS SULLY
American. 1811-1847 and 1783-1872 respectively

Canvas   30⅛ x 25 in.

493   John Randolph
CHESTER HARDING
American. 1792-1866

Canvas   19⅞ x 20½ in.

886   Siegfried and the Rhine Maidens
ALBERT PINKHAM RYDER
American. 1847-1917

FIFTEENTH-CENTURY ITALIAN
SCULPTURE

Terra-cotta   H. $47\frac{9}{16}$ in.

A-1   Madonna and Child
DONATELLO
Florentine. c. 1386-1466

Terra-cotta   H. 19¼ in.

A-19   *Saint John the Baptist*
DONATELLO
Florentine.   c. 1386-1466

Marble   27½ x 18½ in.

A-3   Madonna and Child
DESIDERIO DA SETTIGNANO
Florentine. 1428-1464

Marble   15¾ x 15¾ in.

A-4   *The Young Christ with Saint John the Baptist*
DESIDERIO DA SETTIGNANO
Florentine. 1428-1464

Marble   H. $10\frac{11}{32}$ in.

A-2   Bust of a Little Boy
DESIDERIO DA SETTIGNANO
Florentine. 1428-1464

Marble

H. 17$\frac{15}{32}$ in.

A-8   A Princess of the House of Aragon
FRANCESCO DA LAURANA
Venetian. c. 1425-1502

Marble   28¼ x 22½ in.

A-5   Madonna and Child
Agostino di Duccio
Florentine.   1418-c. 1480

Marble   16¼ x 11¾ in.

A-15   *Madonna and Child*
MINO DA FIESOLE
Florentine. 1431-1484

Marble   H. 49¾ in.

A-6   Charity

MINO DA FIESOLE

Florentine. 1431-1484

Marble   H. 49¾ in.

A-7   Faith
MINO DA FIESOLE
Florentine. 1431-1484

Terra-cotta

H. 24 in.

A-16   Giuliano de' Medici
VERROCCHIO
Florentine. 1435-1488

Terra-cotta   H. 29½ in.

A-17   Putto Poised on a Globe
VERROCCHIO
Florentine. 1435-1488

— 159 —

Marble   Diam. 24 in.

A-9   Lodovico Sforza, Called Il Moro
GIOVANNI ANTONIO AMADEO
Lombard. 1447-1522

Marble

Diam. 24⅜ in.

A-10   Gian Galeazzo Sforza
GIOVANNI ANTONIO AMADEO
Lombard. 1447-1522

Terra-cotta   30¼ x 16¼ in.

A-13   *The Virgin in Adoration*

ANDREA DELLA ROBBIA

Florentine. 1435-1525

Glazed Terra-cotta   35½ x 19 in.

A-12   Madonna and Child with God the Father and Cherubim
ATELIER OF ANDREA DELLA ROBBIA
Florentine. XV Century

Glazed Terra-cotta   Diam. 21½ in.

A-11   Madonna and Child with Cherubim
ATELIER OF ANDREA DELLA ROBBIA
Florentine. XV Century

LATER ITALIAN AND FRENCH SCULPTURE

Bronze   H. 69⅝ in.

A-20   Mercury
GIOVANNI BOLOGNA
Flemish-Florentine. 1524-1608

Bronze   H. 65⅞ in.

A-21   Venus Anadyomene
JACOPO SANSOVINO
Florentine-Venetian. 1486-1570

Bronze   H. 71½ in.

A-22   Bacchus and a Young Faun
Jacopo Sansovino
Florentine-Venetian. 1486-1570

Lead

A-41   Cherubs Playing with a Swan

JEAN BAPTISTE TUBI

Italo-French.   1630/1636-1700

H. 47 in.

Lead

H. 43 in.

A-42   Cherubs with a Lyre

PIERRE LEGROS

French. 1629-1714

Marble   H. 51¾ in.

A-43   Monumental Urn
CLODION (CLAUDE MICHEL)
French. 1738-1814

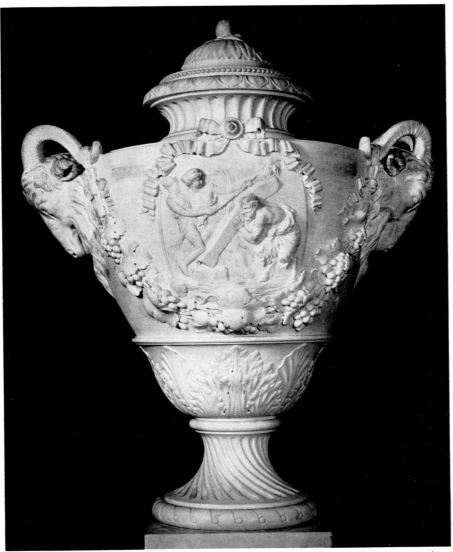

Marble

H. 51¾ in.

A-44   Monumental Urn
CLODION (CLAUDE MICHEL)
French. 1738-1814

LIST OF ARTISTS